A Child's Christmas in San Francisco

A Child's Christmas in San Francisco

John Briscoe

Printed in China by Prolong Press Ltd.

10 9 8 7 6 5 4 3 2 1
FIRST EDITION

iv

For Warren Hinckle

Who would have written this book

But didn't

Contents

Forward, with a Foreword

In San Francisco eating is an art and cooking a science, and he who knows not what San Francisco provides knows neither art nor science. Here have congregated the world's greatest chefs, and when one exclaims in ecstacy [*sic*] over a wonderful flavor found in some dingy restaurant, let him not be surprised if he learn that the chef who concocted the dish boasts royal decoration for tickling the palate of some epicurean ruler of foreign land. . . . This aggregation of cuisinaire, gathered where is to be found a most wonderful variety of food products in the highest state of excellence, has made San Francisco the Mecca for lovers of gustatory delights, and this is why the name of San Francisco is known where men and women sit at table.

—Clarence Edwords, *Bohemian San Francisco**

S an Franciscans have relations with the culinary heritage of their city—Celery Victor, Joe's Special, cioppino—that are intimate to the point of licentious. They are nearly as intimate as a

---

* Clarence Edwords, *Bohemian San Francisco: Its Restaurants and Their Most Famous Recipes* (San Francisco: P. Elder and Co., 1914).

San Franciscan's relations with the city's inventions in the field of drink, which include steam beer, the martini (which we shall visit in "Martini Monday"), and the tiki concoctions of Trader Vic Bergeron. But it took Mel Blanc, the voice of Daffy Duck and Porky Pig, to let us children know, with an audible wink over the radio, that a day in San Francisco belonged to a food, or drink, that originated in San Francisco. For with the *basso profundo* authority of James Earl Jones, Blanc would proclaim, thundering across the airwaves of the old KSFO, the World's Greatest Radio Station (then):

Tuesday . . . is *Red's Tamale Day.*

(Truth be told, listening to him today, Blanc sounds like Bill Dana doing José Jiménez doing Daffy Duck.)

And so, to us, Tuesday was Red's Tamale Day.* "Us" were kids on playgrounds from the North Beach

---

* Blanc also delivered the slogan for Berkeley Farms milk: "Farms–in *Berkeley? Mooo—oooooo.*"

Playground (my front yard) to Grattan in the Upper Haight, Excelsior, Alamo Square, and Dolores Park, and in the yards of the public and parochial grammar schools and the Chinese, Jewish, and other schools spattering our ever-spreading city as we grew.

(Speaking of schools, San Franciscans have a still another strange distinction. Whenever asked by another San Franciscan where we went to school, we know what is meant is not where we went to college, or grammar school, but where we went to high school. The anthem of the ancient and venerable Irish-Israeli-Italian Society of San Francisco even includes this line: "My high school's better than yours cause it's mine." But during this golden age of our doggerel, we were decades from going to high school. The playgrounds and grammar schools were our city-states then.)

Yes, Tuesday was Red's Tamale Day. And in the fullness of time, each other day of the week itself received an assignment, a "pairing" in the current jargon, with a food or drink that had been born in San Francisco. Those pairings were the creative inventions of us San Francisco schoolkids. During the seven days before Christmas, the pairings took on exalted significance. Those days became their own special Advent, especially for those of us who weren't Christian, for reasons so clear then. For the occasion of those seven days, we composed ditties of juvenilia, in verse from bad to worse, to celebrate the days of the week and their paired food or beverage soulmates. From Sutro Heights to South Beach, from Bernal Heights to the Bayview, we composed, and competed, and conceded to the best of us.

San Francisco's playgrounds, and its grammar-school yards, existed then in a pre-Gutenberg, pre-even-papyrus era. Our literary creations reposed in an oral tradition, like Homer's. Most of those creations have been lost to the pyres of time, like Troy itself. Saddest of all, the greatest of our works, the Monday lyrics of an Italian boy from North Beach and a Jewish girl from the Mission, lie buried in the sands of Ocean Beach, figuratively speaking, like shards of the colossal fractured statue of Ozymandias. The lyrics were so clever and quick they would tongue-tie the best players of *Hamilton* today. Only Gino and Esther could recite them. Years later when they were in high school (she attending Lowell, he Galileo) she broke up with him during an hours-long walk on the sand side of the Great Highway seawall, at the end of which they vowed to each other never to recite the Monday poem again. Those Monday lyrics thus disappeared like so much in San Francisco, like the city itself from time to time, like the Maltese Falcon, like Flitcraft, like a fist when you open your hand.

And so, alas for Monday, its second-best poem must be presented here.

Still, this little book draws on the best memories of our city's then-young bards. It is a slim and slender remembrance of but a bit of that dim past. It begins, naturally enough, with Tuesday.

A Child's Christmas in San Francisco

Tuesday is ...

TAMALES

ENCHILADAS

TACOS

TORTILLAS

TACO-ETTES

CHILI CON
  CARNE

CHILI CON
  CARNE WITH
  BEANS

AND REMEMBER:

"Tuesday is RED'S Tamale Day"

... Red's Tamale Day

No one knows anyone who ever ate a Red's Tamale, or admits to it at any rate. Red's Tamales came six to a package, and you could find them in your grocer's freezer case. Each specimen was wrapped in a "husk" that was not a corn husk but a wraith of something suspiciously resembling newsprint that contained, according to accounts, a dollop of a glop of reddish-ness deep within the corn meal slush that lay within the husk. Red's Tamales came in one flavor, red.

For actual tamales you went to Tortola's on Polk Street, Sinaloa on Powell, or, better, Roosevelt Tamale Parlor out on 24th Street, named for a Dutchman who wasn't a President.

Red's
Tamale
Day

Now that Tortola's is closed,

and Sinaloa too,

and unwilling to descend to the level of Red's,

    many of the grownups get hosed.

But Uncle George, so given to gorge, happily ambles

from his 16th and Mission Street Follies

over to the Double Play, for a couple of doubles

and then far down Bryant Street to 24th

for a platter of Roosevelt's chicken tamales.

... **Sourdough Day**

Forty-Niner Howard Gardiner never played a down of football, but he wrote reminiscences of life in the California mines between 1849, the year of the California Gold Rush, and 1857. His book describes the origins of what we call, with characteristic approximation, San Francisco sourdough bread.* (The bread arose—literally—not in San Francisco but in the diggins.) The mixing of water, flour, and yeast had to be in precise proportions, just as the kneading of the dough had to be just enough, and not overmuch. Allowed to rest, and rise, finally the dough was baked, in a Dutch-oven-like kettle buried in coals. The kettle was precious, but not nearly so much as the "starter"—the ball of dough reserved each evening to allow its yeast to grow overnight to be ready to leaven the next day's bake. To protect it

---

* Howard C. Gardiner, *In Pursuit of the Golden Dream: Reminiscences of San Francisco and the Northern and Southern Mines, 1849–1857*, ed. Dale L. Morgan (Stoughton, MA: Western Hemisphere, Inc., 1970), 164–65.

from thieves, the kettle and starter were tucked into bed with their owner, the starter protectively mantled in the pit of the right arm of the miner, who bathed obsessively, sometimes as often as once a month.

Modern explanations for the tang of San Francisco sourdough declare it the fermentation of a "wild San Francisco yeast." Wild yeast my balderdash. *Besame* buncombe, if you buy that.

Sourdough Day

Sour dough requires

    water, yeast, and flour, though

when describing it, do please

    omit the dang

        sine qua non

that gives to the loaf its tang.

Thursday is ...

... Bull Pupp Day

Lugubrious Mexican food was looked to for another day, Thursday.

Playland occupied three city blocks along the Great Highway across from Ocean Beach. It extended from just north of Golden Gate Park and ended where the Great Highway begins its climb to Sutro Heights. An amusement park called Ocean Beach Pavilion existed there since 1884. Amusement park empresario Arthur Looff enlarged the place in 1912 and built Looff's Hippodrome. (No hippos were seen there, though they steamed and snorted in Fleishhacker Zoo just down the Highway.) In 1922 Looff and his partner added a roller coaster, "The Big Dipper," as well as the "Chutes-at-the-Beach" water ride. George Whitney in 1926 became general manager, and the place became known as Whitney's Playland-at-the-Beach. (Whitney purchased the attractions one by one and eventually became owner of the entire park.) Playland included the Funhouse, Skateland, the Wild Mouse, and Laughing Sal (q.v.).

For your dining pleasure, food stands sold Bull Pupp Tacos and Bull Pupp Enchiladas.

In the 1860s Mark Twain wrote an "Earthquake Almanac" for the *San Francisco Dramatic Chronicle* (later, more simply, the *Chronicle*). One entry read, "Occasional shakes, followed by light showers of bricks and plastering. About this time expect more earthquakes, but do not look out for them on account of the bricks." At Playland, when walking beneath the Big Dipper, or beside the Wild Mouse, or while gazing agape at the madness of Queen Sal, one wisely looked out for the occasional hail of Bull Pupp.

Bull
Pupp
Day

You've eaten tacos in Waco

and awakened a wacko.

You've snored in Sonora,

done tea in Tijuana,

but for you nothing beats

   a Bull Pupp enchilada,

with salsa and an *ensalada*

trucked in tinned from Ensenada,

   or some place deep under Fresno.

Friday is ...

PLACES TO DINE
AT THE BEACH

The HOT HOUSE

SPECIALIZING IN ENCHILADAS · TAMALES · TOSTADAS · CHILE RELLENOS
AND OTHER DELICIOUS MEXICAN AND SPANISH DISHES · PREPARED BY
EXPERTS AND SERVED IN THE DELIGHTFUL ATMOSPHERE OF SUNNY MEXICO

The "IT" STAND

FAMOUS FOR PLATE BROILED STEER MEAT HAMBURGERS COOKED
WITHOUT GREASE · AND ELECTRIC GRILLED HOT DOGS CONTAINING
VITAMIN "D" · MADE ESPECIALLY FOR OUR USE · GOOD COFFEE ALWAYS

The PIE SHOP

HOMEMADE PIES & CAKES TURNOVERS · SANDWICHES · FRESH FROZEN
ICE CREAM AND FOUNTAIN SPECIALS · ALL ICE CREAM, PIES & CAKES
SERVED IN WHITNEY BROS. RESTAURANTS AND STANDS ARE MADE HERE

The SEA LION Café

BREAKFASTS · LUNCHES · DINNERS · STEAKS · CHOPS · HAM AND EGGS ·
WAFFLES · HOT OR COLD SANDWICHES · HOME MADE PIES · SPECIAL SUNDAY
DINNERS · THE SEA LION IS A POPULAR PLACE FOR SUNDAY BREAKFASTS

The WAFFLE SHOP

SPECIALIZING IN CREAM WAFFLES · STRAWBERRY AND PECAN WAFFLES
HOT CAKES WITH LITTLE PIG SAUSAGES, BACON OR HAM · STEER
BEEF HAMBURGERS · ELECTRIC GRILLED HOT DOGS · CHOW MEIN · PIES & CAKES

TOPSY'S ROOST

FEATURING THE WORLD'S MOST DELICIOUS FRIED CHICKEN · BAKED HAM ·
CHICKEN PIE · CORN PONES · HOT BISCUITS · WAFFLE FRIED POTATOES ·
AND OTHER DELICIOUS SOUTHERN DISHES · DANCING · PARTIES & BANQUETS

The CLIFF HOUSE

SAN FRANCISCO'S FINEST AND MOST HISTORIC DINING PLACE · SPECIAL
SUNDAY MORNING BREAKFASTS · LUNCHEONS · DINNERS · CUISINE UNEXCELLED ·
BEAUTIFUL MARINE DINING ROOM · NATIVE REDWOOD BAR AND COCKTAIL LOUNGE

... It's-It Day

Grown-ups think children like oatmeal cookies, vanilla ice cream, and thin *faux*-chocolate veneers. Children hate them. Sometimes, though, something synergistical happens with an improbable combination. In 1928, George Whitney, still manager of Playland-at-the-Beach, squeezed a scoop of vanilla ice cream between two oatmeal cookies, dipped the concretion into warm chocolate, and the It's-It Ice Cream Sandwich was born. Playland closed in 1968, and it was demolished in 1972, but in 1974 the It's-It was reborn. Truth be told, it was always good—much better than an Eskimo Pie, a fact that inspired a callow San Francisco boy to compose Friday's poem—on the Friday, no less, of Christmas week. (The poem, one hopes, is particularly appreciated. Its author became a martyr for his art, sentenced to four months of detention after school in penance for it.)

It's-It
Day

An It's-It isn't

a voluptuous Inuit

posing in a thong not

on the Bay of Hong Kong

but on the frozen shore of the Bering Strait

like an idiot.

Saturday is ...

DRINKING PISCO IN A SAN FRANCISCO
SALOON

... Pisco Day

San Francisco's most famous drink is Pisco Punch, first served in Duncan Nichol's Bank Exchange saloon in the Montgomery ("Monkey") Block at the southwest corner of Washington and Montgomery Streets. Both the drink and the bar, which had existed since 1854, survived the earthquake and fire of 1906, but not Prohibition. Oliver Perry Stidger, manager of the Monkey Block and a habitué of the saloon, likened Pisco Punch "to the scimitar of Harroun whose edge was so fine that after a slash a man walked on unaware that his head had been severed from his body until his knees gave way and he fell to the ground dead."*

Pisco has profoundly provoked, by its seductive presence or coy unavailability, artistic productivity in San Francisco. Under the spell of pisco, Frank Norris wrote a novel about a Polk Street dentist so

---

* Doris Muscatine, *Old San Francisco: The Biography of a City from Early Days to the Earthquake* (New York: G. P. Putnam's Sons, 1975), 421.

intensely dark (novels about Polk Street dentists are invariably dark) that it was made into a film three weeks in length called *Greed*. Allen Ginsberg wrote the first lines of "Howl" ("I saw the best minds of my generation destroyed by madness, starving hysterical naked ...") in San Francisco in 1955 while frantically awaiting his delivery of pisco. But the greatest artistic breakthrough occasioned by a pisco debauch, or withdrawal (no one knows which in this particular case), occurred an evening in 1895 when San Francisco poet Gelett Burgess divined that "purple," a word all poets know has no rhyme, rhymed with "pisco." Eschewing the purple-and-pisco rhyme he composed a poem nonetheless, one he claimed he came to loathe, but one that every San Francisco child knows by heart:

> I never saw a purple cow;
> I never hope to see one;
> But I can tell you anyhow
> I'd rather see than be one!*

---

* Burgess wrote serious poetry, and claimed he wished to be known not for "The Purple Cow," but for his "Epic of the Epicures," and "The Cure at Epicurea." But it was "The Purple Cow" that placed him with Homer and Goethe in the celestial pantheon of poets. In exasperation in 1897 he wrote:

After the demise of the Bank Exchange, and of
Nichols, who had obtained the secret recipe from
the original 1854 owners, Pisco Punch disappeared.
Many have claimed to know the true recipe, but the
claims have invariably proved fraudulent. As with
questions such as the origin of life, the immanence
of pi, where Drake landed in 1579, and who wrote
Shakespeare, Pisco Punch has been the subject of
tedious research, and severely serious scholarship.*

Ah yes, I wrote "The Purple Cow" —
I'm Sorry, now, I wrote it,
But I can tell you Anyhow,
I'll Kill you if you Quote it!

Truth be told, Burgess strove to master the difficult art of light verse. The
twenty-four issues of his literary magazine *The Lark* are filled with his light
verses, only one reaching perfection, "The Purple Cow." In private conver-
sation, Joe Parisi, long-time editor of *Poetry* magazine, has asserted that
writing light or nonsense verse is more difficult in some ways than writing
serious verse. One misstep, one false note, and the delicate and intricate
edifice will collapse, whereas in serious verse the reader will forgive a tin
word or halt line, if in succeeding lines the poem recovers its footing, and
wit. Likewise, Kingsley Amis, in the introduction to his *New Oxford Book of
Light Verse*, claimed that light verse writers labor at "the hardest and most
severely technical work known to authorship."

* See, e.g., William Bronson, "Secrets of Pisco Punch Revealed," *Califor-
nia Historical Society Quarterly*, LII (Fall 1973), 229.

Getting
Giddy
Pissed
on
Pisco

Saturday nights in San Francisco

were once

   reserved for a Pisco

Punch nonce.

But the loss for a century of the mystical recipe

   has yet to deter,

however badly he may err,

   even one single barman from serving one once. *

Thomas Knox's *Underground, or Life Below the Surface*, published in 1875, explores life beneath the earth's surface, including the opium dens of nineteenth-century San Francisco, and a quest for Pisco.

> Underground life, of a peculiar and picturesque character, can be seen in San Francisco, in the parts of the city where the Chinese most do congregate. Soon after my arrival there, two of my friends, whom I will call the Doctor and the Colonel, invited me to a nocturnal visit to the Celestials. I accepted with alacrity, and, dressed in my poorest and oldest clothes, met my friends at the appointed hour....

As a "disinfectant," the Colonel suggested, "Pisco?"

"What is Pisco?" I demanded....
   The Colonel took my arm, and as we went down toward Montgomery Street, proceeded, in a confidential manner, to enlighten me on the subject of Pisco.... The first glass satisfied me that San Francisco was, and is, a nice place to visit..... The second glass was sufficient, and I felt that I could face small-pox, all the fevers known to the faculty, and the Asiatic Cholera, combined, if need be.

Kindled with Pisco, the three left on another quest, for "the wine called Cocomongo." Thomas W. Knox, *Underground, or Life Below the Surface* (Hartford: J. B. Burr Publishing Co., 1875), 250–254.

Sunday is ...

Cioppino Day

In 1847 San Francisco (which had just acquired that name) had fewer than five hundred residents, according to a census of that year. Two years later, in the year of the Gold Rush, the city had perhaps a hundred times that number of people (no one knows for sure).

By 1850 nearly eight hundred ships had been abandoned in Yerba Buena Cove, which is now San Francisco's financial district. (Under the lure of riches of gold, the sailors simply abandoned the ships.) One ship, run aground and hemmed in by other abandoned and derelict vessels at the (then watery) intersection of Davis and Pacific Streets, became the city's first Italian waterfront restaurant, owned by Signor Giuseppe Bazzuro of Genoa.* Among Signor Bazzuro's dishes was a fish stew, likely the original cioppino, San Francisco's tomato-bomb version of

---

* Clarence E. Edwards, *Bohemian San Francisco: Its Restaurants and their Most Famous Recipes; The Elegant Art of Dining* (San Francisco: Paul Elder and Company, Publishers, 1914).

bouillabaisse. The fish market in Genoa was called the Chiappa, and in Genovese *cioppin* means fish stew.

On the evening of Christmas Eve, San Francisco children demand cracked crab, until they are served, and taste cioppino.

Not
Days
for
Bouillabaisse

Shoot a man in Reno

    for his winnings at craps and keno,

        and for your last meal, the evening of Christmas Eve

            dispatch your hangman for San Francisco

                for a bib and a bowl of steaming cioppino

                    and a heel of stale sourdough.

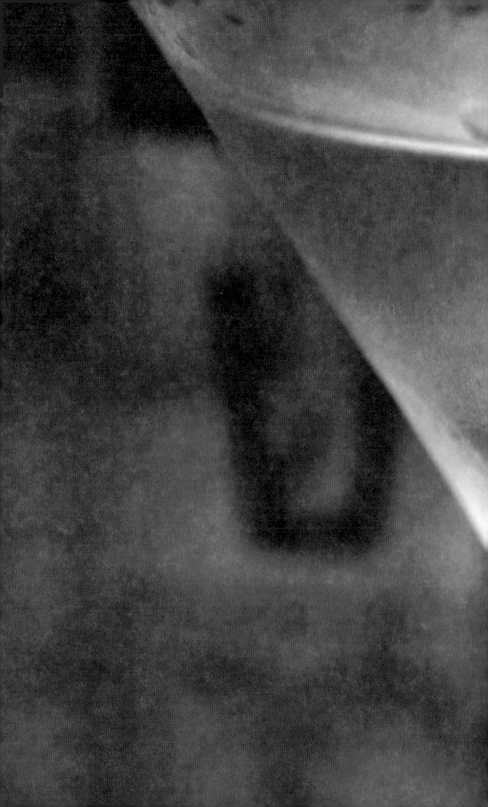

Monday is ...

Martini Day

Let no one perpetuate the myth that the martini was invented in Martinez. Joe and Vince Di-Maggio may have been born in Martinez, but the martini was not.

Nor was it invented in New York at the Knickerbocker Hotel in 1912 by bartender Martini di Arma di Taggia. (That is what Mr. di Arma di Taggia himself claimed—but who could believe *anyone* with such a preposterous name?) The *Oxford English Dictionary* ascribes the name wrongly as deriving from an allusion to Martini & Rossi vermouth. So while the British have their own poppycock version, all accounts, eggshually, save the one true account, are poppycock. The martini was invented in San Francisco. This book stands as authority.*

---

* For an overly objective recitation of the evidence for and against San Francisco as the birthplace of the martini, see Barnaby Conrad III, *The Martini* (San Francisco: Chronicle Books, 1995), 19–25. For the unvarnished truth, see Briscoe (the same), "The Great Martini Fraud," *Argonaut* (Warren Hinckle, ed.) XXVIII, no. 4537 (November 2011).

Martini
Monday

Only because it is Monday

I will have a martini

(my last for a while quite teeny).

Since you are gone it's not a fun day,

so I'll ask for two straws and in that way

pretend it is you holding the other one

   and we are ensconced within

a cream-gilt, posh connubial cabin

of a so-slow boat to Mandalay

   and the martini is really an ice-cream sundae

      spiked with three jiggers of gin.

*

Afterwards, an Afterword

Generations of San Francisco children composed these poems, showing a precocious affection for the culinary tradition and abiding spirits of Christmas in their City of St. Francis. It is curious that the children showed such an interest in alcoholic drinks — perhaps the topic carried the enticing appeal of naughtiness. However that may be, such prominence in the verses of alcoholic drink is, it happens, both an enduring Chinese tradition dating from ancient times, as well as a San Francisco one, and it is tempting to think that in the city East and West met over a shared fondness for libations. Writing more than 1300 years ago Li Po (Li Bai in current rendering), the greatest of Chinese poets, who foretold the establishment of the Chinatown of San Francisco, wrote often of drink and drunkenness.* He went so far in fact as to decree that a bar be built in his name, on Grant Avenue in Chinatown.

Somewhat later, at the turn of the twentieth century, the largest distiller and wholesaler of liquors in San Francisco was A.P. Hotaling, whose wares were housed at 429 Jackson Street. The fire that destroyed most of San Francisco in the four days following the earthquake of April 18, 1906, nearly incinerated Hotaling's warehouses. The earthquake and fire were gleefully cited by persons of the cloth throughout the world as evidence of the incorrigible sinfulness of San Francisco, and the righteous vengeance of the Lord. But in the case of Hotaling's enterprise, Providence Divine, in the form of the United States Navy, intervened. Sailors slung the world's longest fire hose from the waters of the San

---

* For example, "Drinking Alone Beneath the Moon" ("Sober, we're together [that is, the moon, his shadow, and Po himself] and happy . . . / Drunk,/we scatter . . .") and "9/9, Out Drinking on Dragon Mountain," ("Soon drunk, I watch my cap tumble in wind/down Grant Avenue to California Street/ and into the vestibule/of Old St. Mary's Church"), translated in David Hinton, *Classical Chinese Poetry: An Anthology* (New York: Farrar, Straus & Giroux, 2008),179, 185.

Francisco Bay, over Telegraph Hill, down into the Barbary Coast district of San Francisco and there managed miraculously to save Hotaling's stores of liquor. Charley Field then penned* these deathless lines:

> If, as they say, God spanked the town
> For being over-frisky,
> Why did he burn His churches down
> And spare Hotaling's whiskey?

---

* "Penned" is the past tense of an obsolete verb, "pen," a back-formation from the ancient word "pen," which was the noun (thing-word) for a stick-like object with which primitive peoples wrote words (*q.v.*) onto media (*q.v.*) such as paper (*q.v.*).

Merry Christmas, San Francisco.

Too soon

It will be next year again.

Illustrations

Acknowledgments

The author first of all thanks the thousands of San Francisco schoolchildren who so cleverly employed their childhood wits to craft these verses that have withstood the ravages of time and memory. He also gratefully acknowledges Tom Christensen's fastidious editing, artistic design, and his pre-press management of this little book. This is the second time Tom and I have collaborated on a book, and each time gets more fun. Equally fun has been working with Ron Turner and his son Colin on the publication of the book. And of course I must thank our departed great friend Warren Hinckle, for not having written it first.

About the Author

John Briscoe is a San Francisco poet, author, and lawyer. His poetry has been praised by *Kirkus Review*, *Columbia*, and many other reviews. His book *Crush: The Triumph of California Wine* took the Oscar Lewis Award in western history for 2020, and first prize in the Top Shelf Book Awards. As a lawyer, he has tried and argued cases throughout the country, and in the United States Supreme Court and the Permanent Court of Arbitration in The Hague. He is a Distinguished Scholar at the University of California, Berkeley, president of the San Francisco Historical Society, and co-owner of venerable Sam's Grill in San Francisco.

This book was published by Last Gasp Press, San Francisco, under the direction of Ron Turner and Colin Turner. It was edited, designed, and typeset in Scala Pro and Scala Sans Pro by Thomas Christensen, and printed in China by Prolong Press, Ltd. on LPHJ 180 gsm creamy woodfree paper.